Mel Bay Presents

Four Centuries of
Women Composers

by Gail Smith

1 2 3 4 5 6 7 8 9 0

Visit us on the Web at www.melbay.com — E-mail us at email@melbay.com

Table of Contents

Marie Antoinette

Archduchess of Austria, Queen of France
(1755-1793)

She was born in Vienna on November 2, 1755. Marie studied with the famous composer Gluck in Vienna. She was a harpist and composed many songs. During the French Revolution, Marie Antoinette was guillotined and died October 16, 1793 in Paris.

'Tis My Friend

Queen Marie Antoinette
Arr.by Gail Smith

Madame Dussek

(Sophia Corri Dussek)
(1775 - 1830)

Sophia was born in Edinburgh, Scotland in 1775. Her father, Domenico Corri, taught her to play the piano at an early age. Sophia was a child prodigy who sang and played the piano in public at the age of four. In 1788 her family moved to London. She gave her first concert there at Hanover Square in April 1791. Sophia sang in many concerts arranged by Salomon to promote Joseph Haydn. Sophia married the Czech pianist, Jan Ladislav Dussek in 1792. In 1800 her husband deserted her and left the country after his business failed. After he died in 1812, Sophia married John Moralt. They established a music school in Paddington for piano students. Her compositions include a Sonata for piano, Opus 1; Three Sonatas for Harp and several other pieces. This Rondo was published by Natale Corri in the Second Collection of Admired Marches, Waltzes, Minuets & Airs in Edinburgh; circa 1815. This book is in the library of Gail Smith.

Rondo

Sophia Dussek

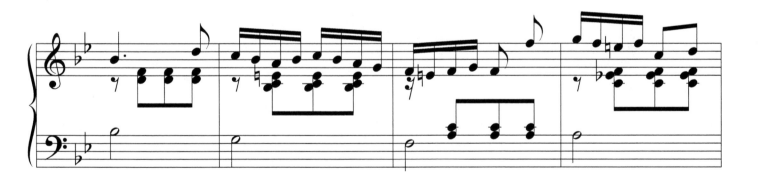

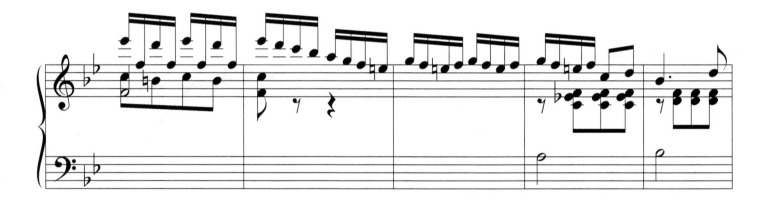

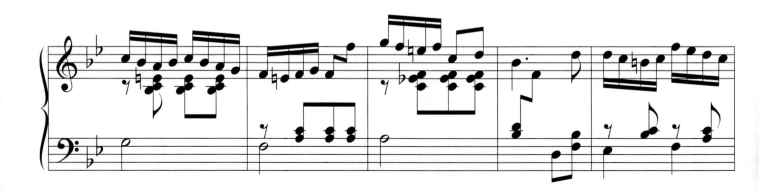

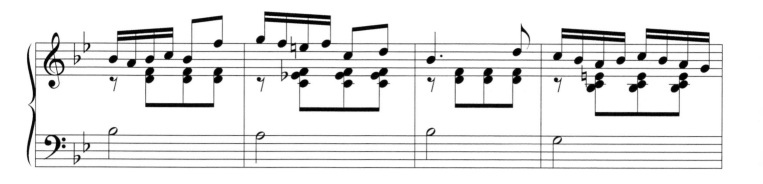

Coda

Fine

This page has been left blank
to avoid awkward page turns.

Fanny Cecile Mendelssohn Hensel

(1805 - 1847)

Fanny Cecile Mendelssohn Hensel was born November 14, 1805, in Hamburg, Germany. Fanny was a child prodigy who grew up in a wealthy family. Her mother began teaching her piano along with her brother Felix, who was four years younger than Fanny. By the time she was thirteen years old, Fanny could play the entire Well-tempered Clavier by J. S. Bach by memory! Her brother Felix began to perform in public at age nine and was composing when he was eleven.

Although Felix was in the limelight, Fanny kept up her musical study alongside her brother. In the publication "Songs Without Words," composed by her brother, are six of Fanny's compositions: Op. 8, Nos. 2, 3, and 12, and Op. 9, Nos. 7, 10, and 12. She composed those six songs under his name because Felix liked them so much. Fanny published four books of melodies in her own name and also composed a lovely piano trio. Many of her works still remain unpublished. She composed over 400 works.

On October 3, 1829, Fanny married the Prussian court painter Wilhelm Hensel. He encouraged her composing, but it was her brother Felix who was opposed to her pieces being published. Fanny only played once in public, at a charity event, in 1838. It simply was not proper in those days for women to perform in public. Fanny was a leading participant at the family's private Sunday afternoon concert series.

Fanny and Felix were extremely close. Felix valued her judgment and musical advice and often said that she played better than he did. She constantly promoted his work. Fanny died suddenly while rehearsing a performance of his Walpurgisnacht in the family auditorium on May 17, 1847, in Berlin, Germany. Felix fainted when he heard of her death and never regained his full energy. He died six months later. A theme of her music is engraved on the tombstone where she is buried.

Übungsstück

Fanny Mendelssohn Hensel

Allegro moderato

Fine

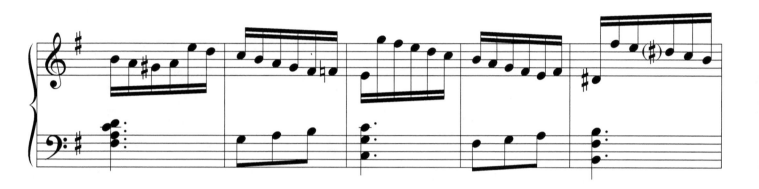

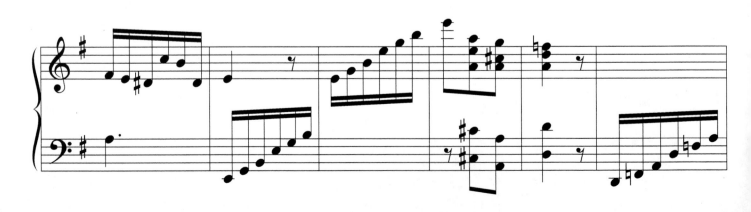

D. C. al Fine

This page has been left blank
to avoid awkward page turns.

Clara Schumann

(1819 - 1896)

Clara Wieck Schumann was born on September 13, 1819 in Leipzig, Germany. Her father was a famous music teacher and composer. He was her piano teacher and began teaching her at an early age. She gave her first concert at the age of nine. By the time Clara was eighteen, she was second only to Franz Liszt among European pianists. Clara was the first to introduce Chopin's music to Germany; the first to play the Appassionata Sonata by Beethoven in Vienna on January 7, 1838; and the first to introduce many of Robert Schumann's works to the public.

Robert Schumann took piano lessons from Clara's father. Clara and Robert became friends, and as she grew older their friendship blossomed into love. Her father opposed the thought of marriage. A long struggle continued until she was of legal age. Mr. Wieck said, "If Clara married Schumann, I would say upon my deathbed that she is not worthy to be called my daughter." Finally, Robert and Clara married without her father's consent on September 12, 1840, the day before her twenty-first birthday. The wedding was at ten o'clock in the morning in a little country church at Schonefield. Only Clara's mother and their faithful friend Ernst Becker, came with them. After they were married by the minister, the carriage drove them back to town, where a privileged group of friends were waiting to greet them.

Robert composed many beautiful piano works for his wife to perform. After the successful performance of his First Symphony and the arrival of their first child, Clara's father wrote them a letter of conciliatory words. During Christmas of 1843, Robert and Clara visited him for a family reunion.

Clara managed to continue her piano concerts and raise seven children. One child died in infancy and three adult children predeceased her. Clara composed many songs that she dedicated to her husband, Robert. After her husband's death, she edited his works for publication and performed them in concerts. Clara died on May 20, 1896, about forty years after her husband's death.

Toccatina

Clara Schumann
Opus 6

*) Note in the first edition (in French): Proper use of the pedal is presupposed, and is
written out only in the most necessary passages.

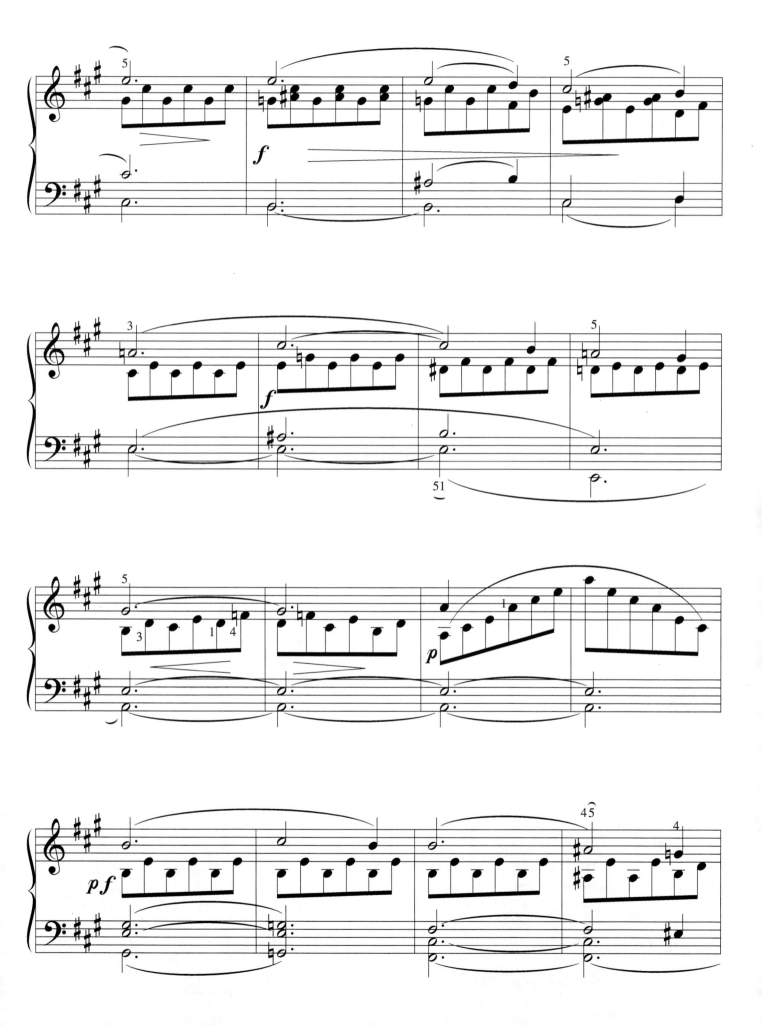

Tempo I

This page has been left blank
to avoid awkward page turns.

Clara Gottschalk Peterson

Clara was the sister of the famous composer, Louis Gottschalk. Their father was Edward Gottschalk, a London Jewish man who came to America and settled in New Orleans around 1820. He became a successful land speculator and married fifteen year old Marie Aimee de Brusle of Catholic faith from Louisiana. When their father died, bankrupt, in 1853, Louis assumed his father's debt's and supported his mother, his sister Clara and four other siblings. Their mother died in 1856.

After her brother Louis' death in 1870, Clara compiled her brother's diary, letters and numerous articles. She published a collection called "Notes of a Pianist". (In 1984, the New York Public Library for the performing Arts at Lincoln Center acquired this historic collection assembled by Clara.) Aside from promoting her brother, Clara composed many songs including "Creole Songs from New Orleans in the Negro Dialect" (New Orleans L. Grunewald Co., 1909). The piano solo, "In Sylvan Glade" was published in The Etude Magazine, January 1908.

In Sylvan Glade

Dans La Clairiere
Bluette Mazurka

Moderato e grazioso M. M.

Clara Gottschalk Peterson
Opus 26

Pomposo

37

This page has been left blank
to avoid awkward page turns.

Queen Liliuokalani

(1838 - 1916)

Queen Liliuokalani composed hundreds of songs, sang and played the guitar. Queen Liliuokalani was born September 2, 1838 and died November 11, 1916. She went to school at the age of four and was well-educated. Liliuokalani spoke English, learned French and later German. She was descended from two famous chiefs who helped make the Hawaiian Islands into a united system. Her name, Lydia Kamakaeha, was changed to Liliuokalani when she assumed her duties as queen. This name means "The Salt Air of Heaven" or "One Belonging to Heaven and of Chiefly Rank."

On September 16, 1862 Liliuokalani married John Owens Dominis, an Italian who moved to Hawaii in 1837. Dominis and his father were traders from Boston who built a lovely colonial home on Honolulu which is known as "Washington Place." This is where Liliuokalani lived from 1898 until her death. Her husband became governor of Oahu Island in 1863, an office he held until August, 1891, when he died.

In her book *Hawaii's Story* by Hawaii's Queen Liliuokalani writes:

> In my school days my facility in reading music at sight was always recognized.... After leaving school, my musical education was continued from time to time as opportunity offered, but I scarcely remember the days when it would not have been possible for me to write either the words or the music for any occasion on which poetry or song was needed. To compose was as natural to me as to breathe. I have never yet numbered my compositions, but am sure they must run well up to the hundreds. Of these not more than a quarter have been printed. Even when I was denied the aid of an instrument, I could transcribe to paper the tones of my voice.

In the autumn of 1874 King Kalakaua, Liliuokalani's brother became king and visited America to sign a treaty which gave Pearl Harbor to the United States. Liliuokalani wanted Hawaii to be a sovereign power and strongly opposed this signing.

In 1887 Liliuokalani went to England as the guest of Queen Victoria for the Fiftieth Jubilee celebration. When her brother suddenly died on January 29, 1891, she became the Queen on the throne. Queen Liliuokalani attempted to form a new constitution that would have restored voting rights to the Hawaiian people. She abdicated on January 24, 1895 after four years of turbulence. Liliuokalani then became a private citizen.

"Aloha Oe" was composed by Queen Liliuokalani at Haunawili in 1878 and first performed by the Royal Hawaiian Band. It is a Hawaiian greeting meaning "Love to you."

Aloha Oe

Queen Lilivokalani
arr. by Gail Smith

43

Teresa Carreno

(1853 -1917)

Teresa Carreño was a famous child prodigy who dazzled America in the late nineteenth century. Teresa played the piano at the White House for President Abraham Lincoln when she was only ten years old. Her life story is filled with drama. She was a prima donna who tried to mix marriage and music. Teresa was the mother of four children and was married four times. Her husbands were: Emile Saurel (June 1873); Giovanni Tagliapietra (1876); Eugene d'Albert (1892-95); and Arturo Tagliapietra (June 30, 1902). After one of her concerts a critic was quoted, "Frau Carreño, yesterday played for the first time the second concerto of her third husband in the fourth Philharmonic Concert."

Teresa Carreño's concert schedule took her around the globe. During her summer vacations, Carreño often taught talented students who idolized her. There wasn't much time left after teaching and practicing for her concerts, however, she managed to compose some wonderful music. Her works include: a String Quartet; Petite danse for orchestra; 39 concert pieces for piano and a waltz,"Mi Teresita", named after her daughter. Carreño kept very busy. On the average, Carreño gave 70 concerts a year, traveling from one city to another. Teresa performed Grieg's piano concerto and actually knew Grieg. She performed Edward MacDowell's Piano Concerto and yes, she not only knew him, she had been his piano teacher! The composer, pianist Amy Beach, dedicated the only piano concerto she composed to none other than Teresa Carreño. Everyone wanted Teresa to perform their works in her numerous concerts around the world. Teresa spoke five languages fluently.

Teresa Carreño was born in Caracas, Venezuela on December 22, 1853. Her father Manuel Antonio Carreño, was an excellent pianist and began teaching her when she was four years old. Manuel wrote 500 exercises that covered all the technical and rhythmical difficulties any pianist would encounter. Gradually she learned them all and could play them in rotation every three days in any key. Her father, Manuel Antonio, was the Minister of Finance in Venezuela.

In 1862 the Carreño family was driven from Venezuela by a revolution and sailed to America settling in New York. The family fortune had been left in Venezuela to a trusted friend who was administrating the property for them. His sudden death became a catastrophe for the Carreño family. The dishonest son pretended to know nothing about the funds that had been placed in trust with his father which also included the grandmother's small fortune. The Carreño household numbered fourteen counting the children and servants. The father realized that they only had enough money to last a month. Teresa was always being asked to give a concert, so her father decided that he would consent to his daughter playing the piano in public for money.

Teresa's first concert was a success and the momentum produced more soon after. For her encores, Teresa would play "Gottschalk's Waltz", which she composed when only eight years old. Teresa composed this lovely piece to honor the famous concert pianist Gottschalk who gave her several piano lessons. A busy life began for Teresa from then on. Sometimes she would give two concerts a day in and around Boston. Teresa practiced new pieces for her repertoire and composed new songs to play as well. Teresa came up with the idea to give a matinee concert for children. Soon other cities called for concerts. Her career had begun and would last 55 years.

When Teresa was twelve years old her father brought her to Paris for further study. She auditioned at the Paris Conservatory and was refused admission because she had already gone beyond their requirements for graduation. Teresa studied with Georges Matthias, a pupil of Chopin, and later with Rubinstein.

Teresa's career included her performance as an opera singer. She is remembered as the most talented composer, concert pianist, and child prodigy in musical history. Teresa is the only woman composer on a postage stamp. Teresa's final concert was in Havana on March 21, 1917. She died in New York on June 12, 1917.

Gottschalk Waltz

Performed by Teresa with great success at her Concerts in America.

Teresa Carreño

INTRODUCTION

Andante

con espressione

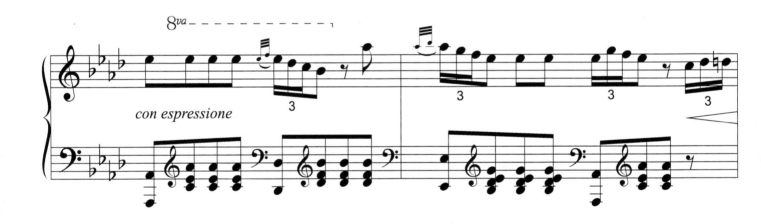

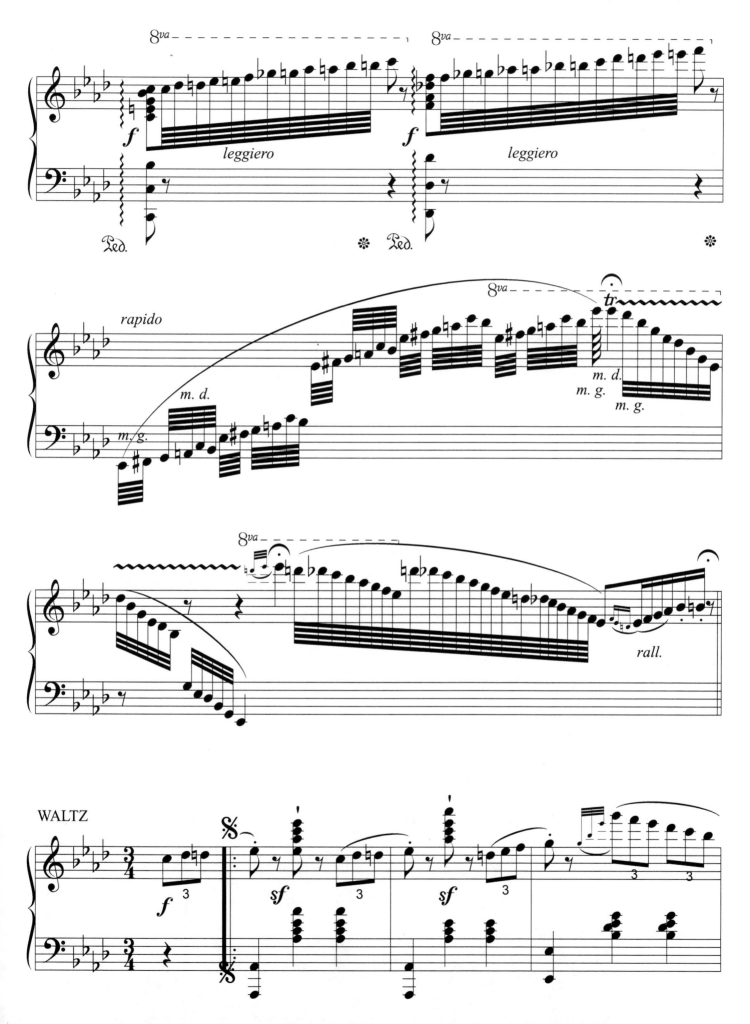

48

scherz.

poco a poco cresc.

dolce

53

con espressione

cresc. _ _ _

Dal Segno al Fine

54

CODA

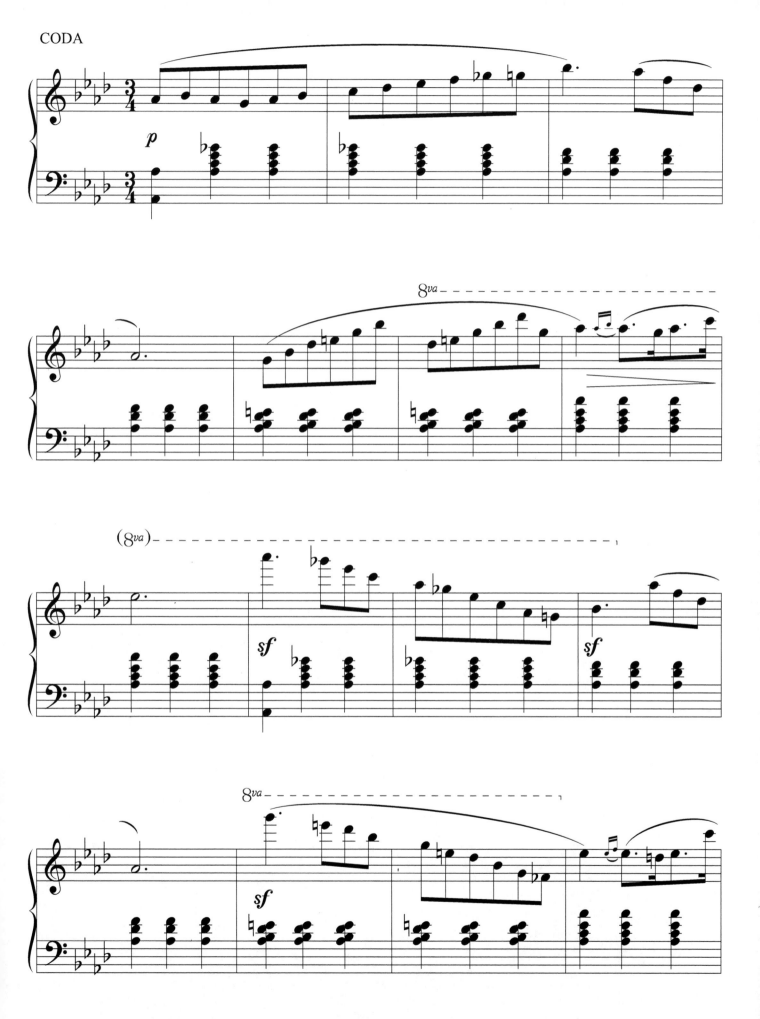

Caprice - Polka

Teresa Carreno
Op. 2

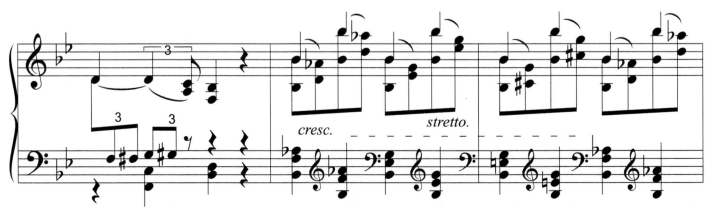

59

Tranquillo.

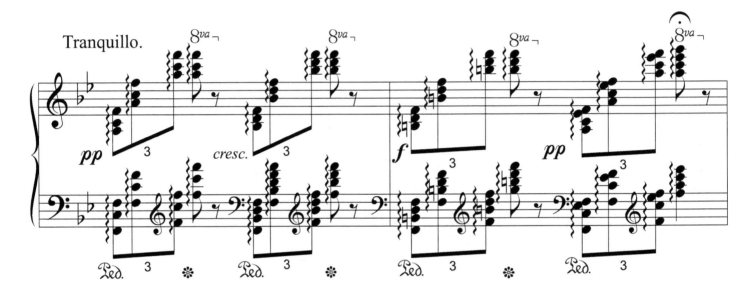

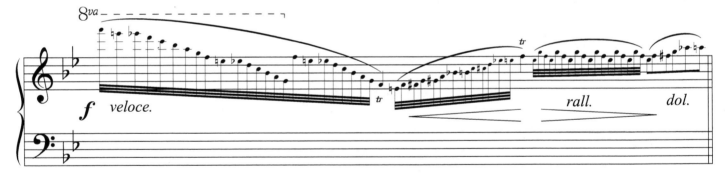

Allegro Tempo di Polka.

70

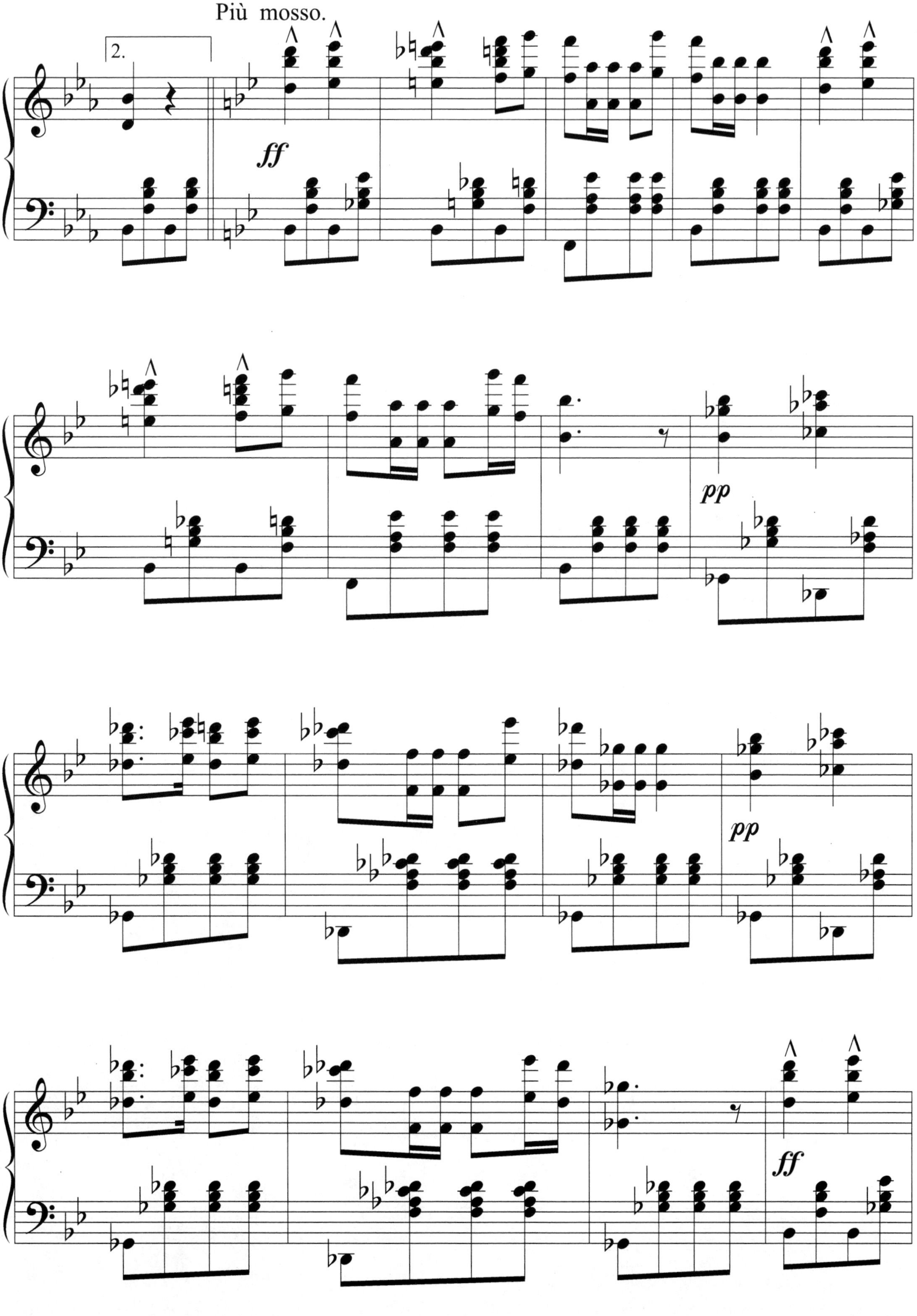

Più mosso.
2.
ff
pp
pp
ff

Cecile Chaminade

(1857 - 1944)

Cecile Chaminade was born in Paris on August 8, 1857. She grew up in a musical household where her parents and their friends played trios and quartets and her sister sang. When she was eight years old, the famous French composer Bizet visited the Chaminade home. Cecile played one of her compositions for him, and he was amazed. Her parents took his advice and found her the best teachers in Paris. Cecile studied with Le Couppey, Savart, and Benjamin Godard. She composed some church music as a child.

When Cecile was eighteen years old, she gave her first public concert and then began touring all over Europe. Cecile performed many of her own works in her concerts. She composed over two hundred piano pieces, yet her most famous piece is the lovely Scarf Dance, Op. 37, No.3, which sold millions of copies.

She made her American debut in 1908 with the Philadelphia Orchestra, performing her Concertstück of 1896. Cecile was one of the first women to make a career of composing, and she also appeared as a conductor. Cecile died in Monte Carlo April 13, 1944.

Gavotte

C. Chaminade
Op.9, No. 2

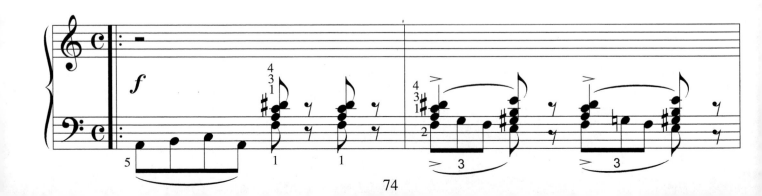

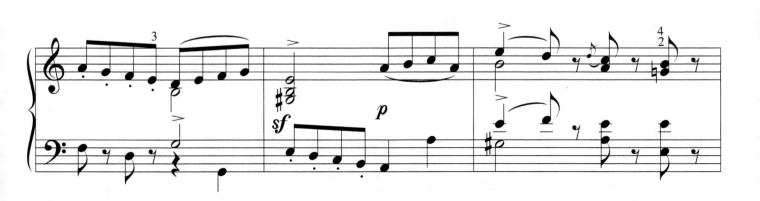

Amy Marcy Beach

(1867-1944)

Amy Marcy Beach was born in Henniker, New Hampshire, on September 5, 1867. Her mother was her first piano teacher. Amy was a child prodigy, who composed her first song at the age of four. She was very sound sensitive and heard music in colors. To Amy, the key of E-flat was pink, and the key of Ab was blue. She accurately notated the bird songs for a famous scientist when she was just ten years old. Amy remained interested in bird songs all her life and composed "The Hermit Thrush at Morn" after hearing one sing outside her window at the MacDowell Colony one summer.

Amy made her debut at the age of sixteen with the Boston Symphony Orchestra. When she was eighteen she married Dr. H. H. A. Beach, a wealthy doctor who was older than her father. They had a happy twenty-five-year marriage, during which time Amy composed most of her major orchestral works.

Amy composed the piano Concerto in C-sharp minor, the Gaelic Symphony, numerous vocal solos, choral anthems, chamber works, cantatas, and hundreds of piano solos. Amy performed her concerto all over the world and concertized throughout the United States.

She died in New York City on December 27, 1944. Her great music lives on to inspire us. The following is a quote from Mrs. H. H. A. Beach: The First Woman Composer of America: "The monuments of a nation mark the progress of civilization, but its intelligence and education are qualified by its music."

Columbine.

Mrs. H. H. A. Beach
Op. 25. No. 2

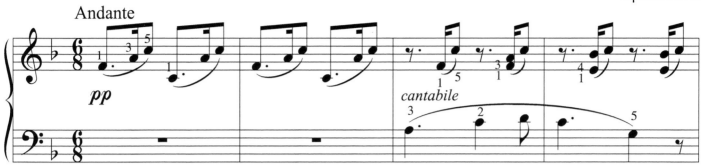

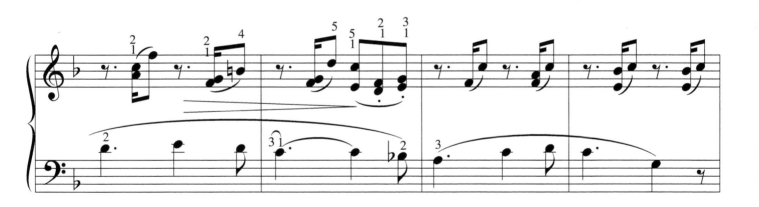

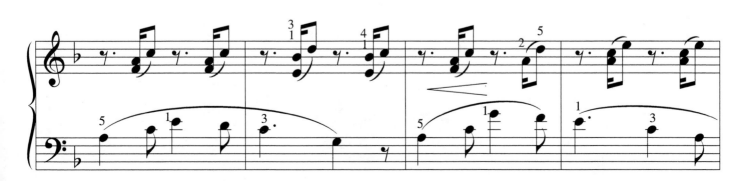

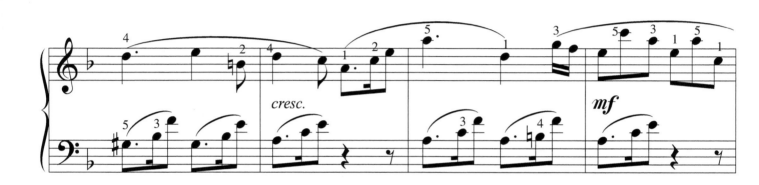

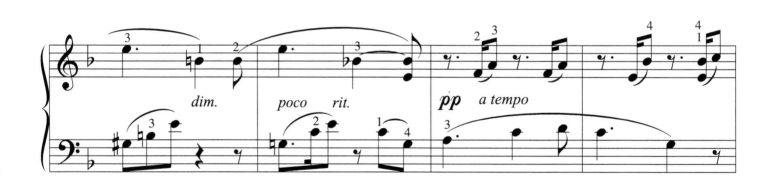

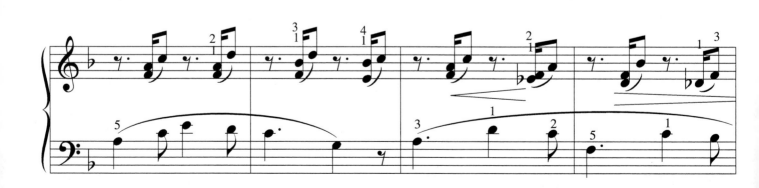

di - mi - nu - en - do e

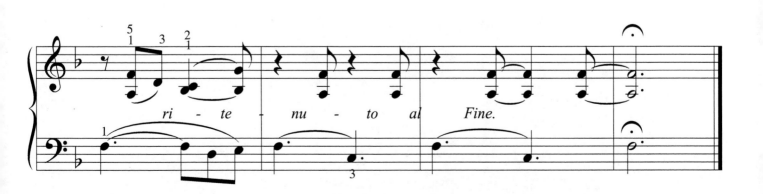

ri - te - nu - to al Fine.

Pantalon.

Mrs. H. H. A. Beach
Op. 25. No. 3

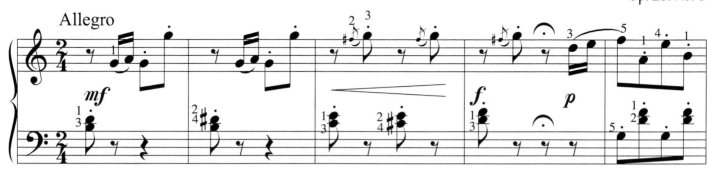

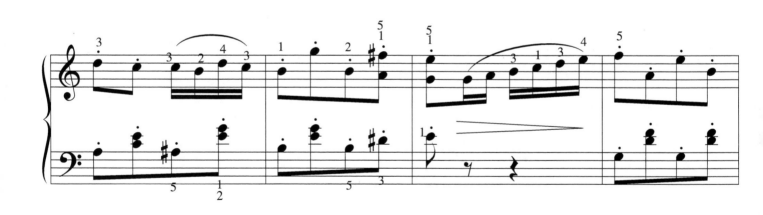

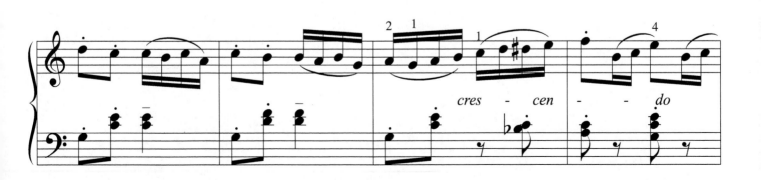

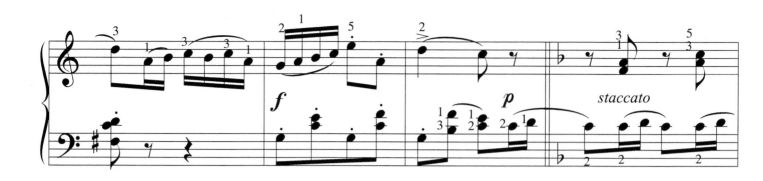

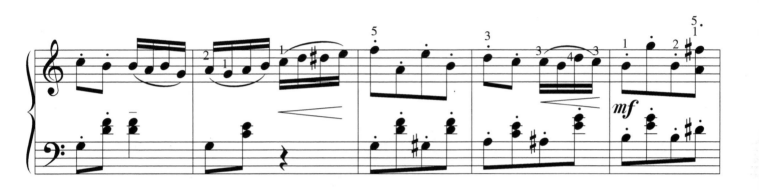

Barcarolle

Mrs. H. H. A. Beach
Op. 28. No. 1

con molto espressione

cresc.

Ped.

4   1   3

f

dim.

Ped.   Ped.

93

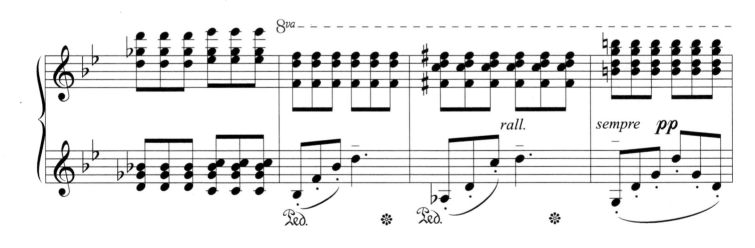

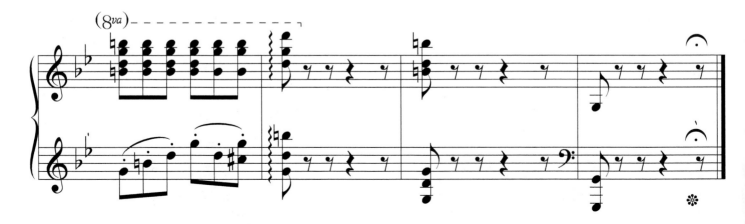

Gail Smith

Author Gail Smith was born in Bridgeport, Connecticut, on January 26, 1943. All of her grandparents were born in Sweden. Gail's father, Carl Erick Johnson, sang tenor in the church choir. Her mother, Ethel, played the piano and had Gail start piano lessons.

Gail Smith received her Bachelor of Fine Arts degree from Florida Atlantic University. She has taught piano students from the age of 3 to 99! Her blind student, Ivan, was seen on national TV.

Giving musical lecture recitals by portraying the composer has been an effective way to reach audiences with the history of music. Gail has portrayed Marian MacDowell and Anna Magdalena Bach. She gives many workshops and concerts throughout the States as well as in Germany and Japan.

Gail has two daughters and is married to C. Alonza Smith. They live in Fort Lauderdale, Florida. Her life has revolved around her family, church and music. Gail has been the pianist of the famed

Coral Ridge Presbyterian church for many years. She has been active in many organizations including being national music chairman of the NLAPW and President of the local branch. She is a member of The Freedoms Foundation of Valley Forge, National Music Teachers Association, and Federation of Music Clubs.

Gail's works include many piano solos, choral works, a piano trio, a composition for four pianist and numerous vocal solos. She has arranged hundreds of hymns, Indian melodies, and folk tunes from many countries. Gail has composed twelve piano palindromes, which are her trademark. These unique solos can be played backwards as well as forwards and sound the same.

Other Books of interest by Gail Smith are: "Great Women Composers", "The Life and Music of Amy Beach", "The Complete Church Pianist", "Celebrate The Piano Series", The Great Literature Series "Twelve Spirituals for Piano Solo", "Palindromes", and "The Complete Book of Improvisation, Fills and Chord Progressions".

Golden Sonata

Gail Smith

Andante con espressivo

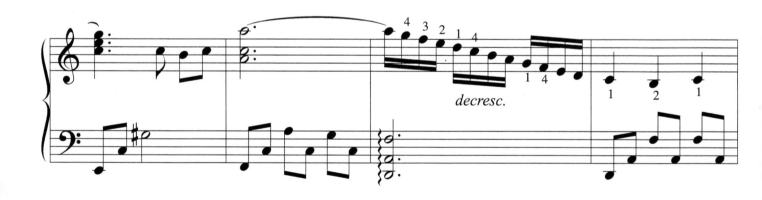

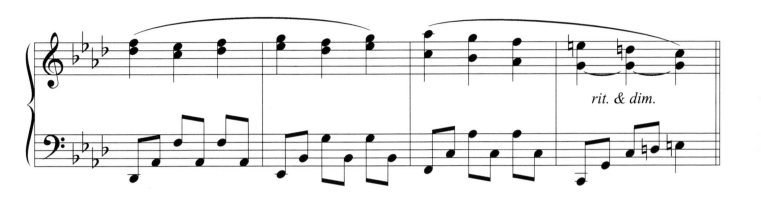

rit. & dim.

Tranquil

mp

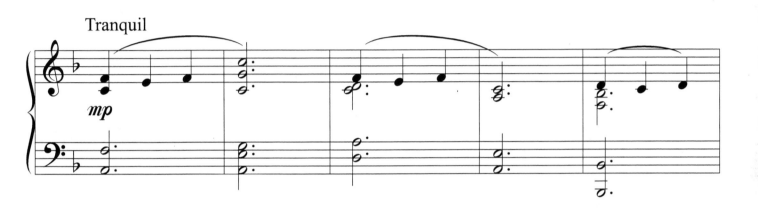

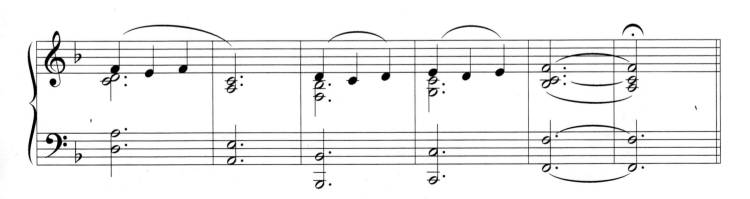

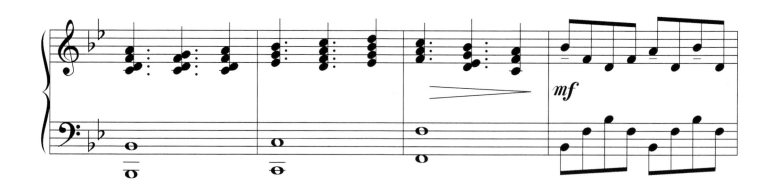

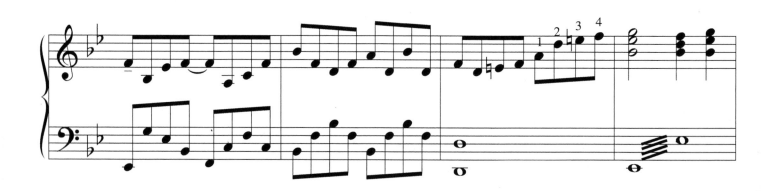

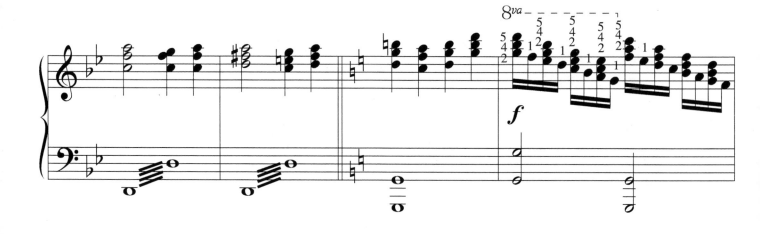

Maestoso.

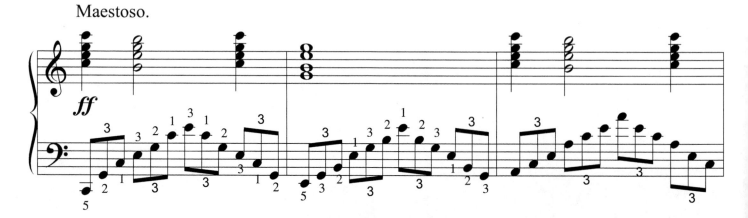

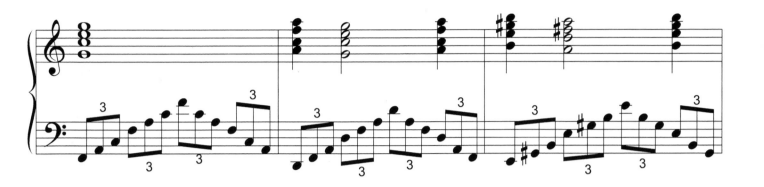

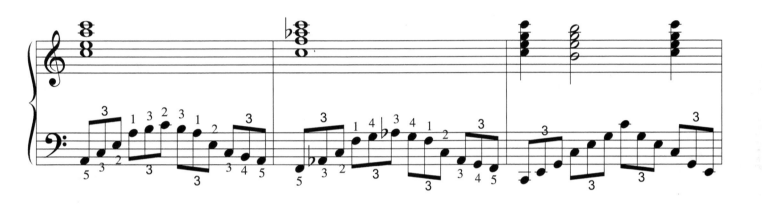

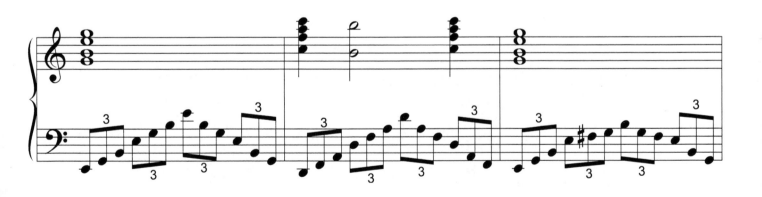

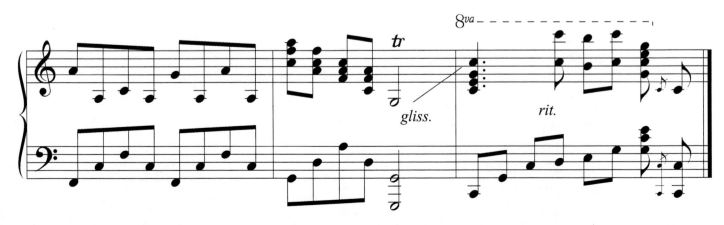

Arlynne
Dedicated to Arlynne Vollmuth

Gail Smith

Andante expressivo

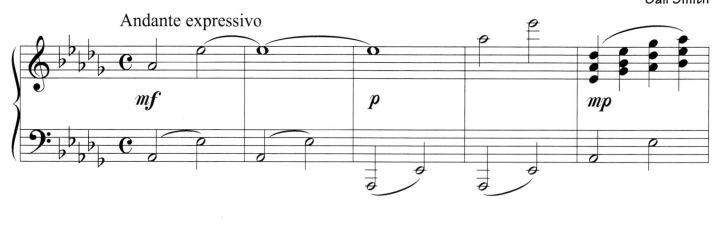

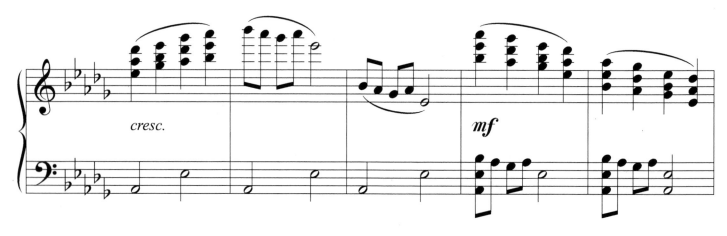

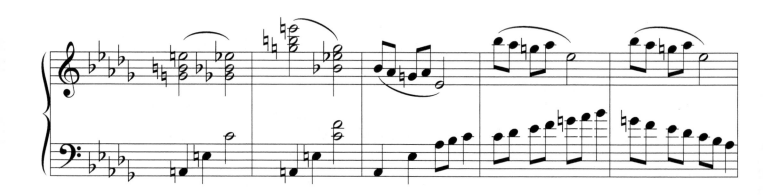

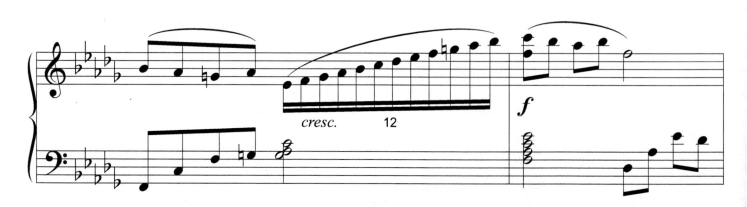

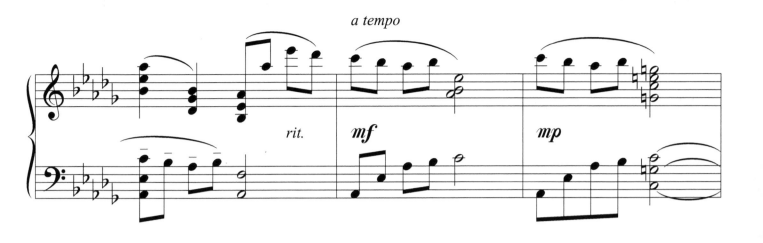

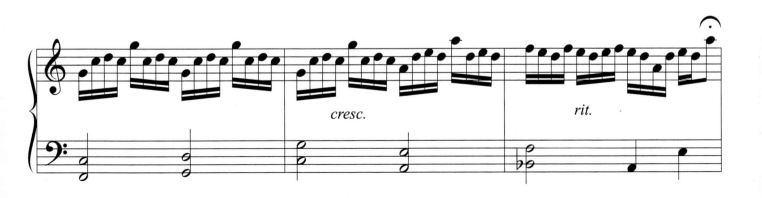

This page has been left blank
to avoid awkward page turns.

Dedicated to Sandy and Tori

Memories

Gail Smith

108